Happiness is an Inside Job

humor and wisdom for living and loving life

PuddleDancer PRESS™

Created by Meiji Stewart

Illustrated by David Blaisdell

Happiness is an Inside Job
© 1997 by Meiji Stewart

ISBN# 0-9647349-8-2

PuddleDancer Press is an imprint of the
Keep Coming Back Company.
Published in Del Mar, California
P.O. Box 1204, Del Mar, California 92014
1-800-522-3383

1st Printing

Illustration: David Blaisdell, Tucson, Arizona
Cover design: Kahn Design, Encinitas, California
Book design: Roger Krueger, San Diego, California
Printing: Dickinson Press, Grand Rapids, Michigan

Dedicated to my family, who mean the world to me:
My mother, Nanette, and father, Richard, my grandmother
Mary, my sister, Leslie, my brothers, Ray and Scott, my
nephews and nieces Sebastien, Emilie, Skye, Luke, Jake,
Nanette, Cairo and Kamana, and to Fumi, Jocelyne, Richard
and Stephen. And especially to my daughter Malia (the
puddledancer), and her loving mom, Julie.

Thanks to:
David for the wonderful illustrations. I am truly blessed to be
able to work with him. Thanks also to Roger for putting it all
together, almost always under deadline (usually yesterday).
Thanks to Jeff for the delightful book covers, and, even more,
for his friendship. Thanks to Zane, Regina, Jan, Gay and Jane
for all you do and for being so loving and caring. And a very
special thanks to my mom and dad for encouraging me to
believe in and pursue my dreams.

It is the inalienable right of all to be happy.

Elizabeth Cady Stanton

Joy is what happens to us when
we allow ourselves to recognize
how good things really are.

Marianne Williamson

Happiness is like jam; you can't spread even a little without getting some on yourself. *Vern McLellan*

The World is a great mirror. It reflects back to
you what you are. If you are loving, if you
are friendly, if you are helpful, the World will
prove loving and friendly and helpful to you.
The World is what you are.

Thomas Dreier

Gratitude is being more aware of
what you have than what you don't.
Recognizing the treasure in the simple—
a child's hug, fertile soil, a golden sunset.

The supreme happiness of life is the
conviction that we are loved. *Victor Hugo*

If you don't enjoy what you have,
how could you be happier with more?

Real happiness is cheap enough,
yet how dearly we pay for its counterfeit.

Hosea Ballou

You can't have everything. Where would you put it? *Steven Wright*

Life's a pretty precious and wonderful thing. You can't sit down and let it lap around you... you have to plunge into it; you have to dive through it! And you can't save it, you can't store it up; you can't horde it in a vault. You've got to taste it; you've got to use it. The more you use, the more you have... That's the miracle of it!

Kyle Chrichton

Not what we have, but what we enjoy constitutes our abundance.

J. Petit-Senn

Do not worry about whether or not the
sun will rise. Be prepared to enjoy it.

Little by little
the time goes by,
short if you sing it,
long if you sigh.

You whose day it is,
make it beautiful.
Get out your rainbow colors,
so it will be beautiful.

Song to Bring Fair Weather, Nootka

Life is short. Eat dessert first.

H. Bland

What time is it? Time to do well, Time to live better,
Give up that grudge, Answer that letter,
Speak the kind word to sweeten a sorrow,
Do that kind deed you would leave 'till tomorrow.

To carry a grudge is like
being stung to death by one bee.

William H. Walton

Warning! Carrying a grudge can be harmful to your health. *Meiji Stewart*

Often people attempt to live their lives backwards: they try to have more things, or more money, in order to do more of what they want so that they will be happier. The way it actually works is the reverse. You must first be who you really are, then, do what you need to do, in order to have what you want.

Margaret Young

Each day comes bearing its gifts.
Untie the ribbons.

Ann Schabacker

This is a record of your time. This is your movie. Live out your dreams and fantasies. Whisper questions to the sphinx at night. Sit for hours at sidewalk cafes and drink with your heroes. Make pilgrimages to Mougins and Abiquiu. Look up and down. Believe in the unknown for it is there. Live in many places. Live with flowers and music and books and painting and sculpture. Keep a record of your time. Learn to read well. Learn to listen and speak well. Know your country, know your world, know your history, know yourself. Take care of yourself physically and mentally. You owe it to yourself. Be good to those around you. And do all of these things with passion. Give all that you can. Remember, Life is short and Death is long.

Fritz Shoulder

It's only when we truly know and understand that
we have a limited time on earth—and that we
have no way of knowing when our time is up—
that we will begin to live each day to the fullest,
as if it was the only one we had.

Elisabeth Kubler-Ross

Take the trip. Purchase the gift. Do it.
The seized opportunity renders joy.

Max Lucado

For better or worse, you must play your own little
instrument in the orchestra of life. *Dale Carnegie*

Scatter seeds of kindness everywhere you go; scatter bits of courtesy—watch them grow and grow. Gather buds of friendship; keep them till full-blown; you will find more happiness than you have ever known.

Amy R. Raabe

I don't know what your destiny will be, but one thing I know: the only ones among you who will be truly happy are those who will have sought and found a way to serve.

Albert Schweitzer

One person can make a difference and every person should try. *John F. Kennedy*

If we want a joyous life, we must think joyous thoughts. If we want a prosperous life, we must think prosperous thoughts. If we want a loving life, we must think loving thoughts. Whatever we send out mentally or verbally will come back to us in like form.

Louise L. Hay

For just a brief while every day,
I steal away from duty.
And leave the indoor tasks undone,
To keep a tryst with beauty.

Mary Scott Fitzgerald

Life is painting a picture, not doing a sum.
Oliver Wendall Holmes

Choose the way of life. Choose the way
of love. Choose the way of caring. . .
Choose the way of goodness.
It's up to you. It's your choice.

Leo Buscaglia

The greatest discovery of my generation
is that a human being can alter
his life by altering his attitudes.

William James

Any life truly lived is a risky business, and if one puts up too may fences against the risks one ends by shutting out life itself. *Kenneth S. Davis*

Learn to get in touch with silence within yourself and know that everything in this life has a purpose. There are no mistakes, no coincidences, all events are blessings given to us to learn from.

Elizabeth Kubler-Ross

Your diamonds are not in far distant mountains or in yonder seas; they are in your own backyard, if you but dig for them.

Russell H. Conwell

Happiness is inside. Inquire within.

Every morning is a fresh beginning.
Every day is the world made new.
Today is a new day.
Today is my world made new.
This is my day of opportunity.

Dan Custer

Take time to notice how
amazing your world truly is.

Aerodynamically the bumble bee shouldn't be able to fly, but the bumble bee doesn't know it so it goes on flying anyway. *Mary Kay Ash*

Friends Are...

Amazing, cherish them. • Blessings, acknowledge them. Caring, appreciate them. • Dependable, rely on them. Encouraging, hear them. • Fallible, love them. • Gifts, unwrap them. • Healing, receive them. • Important, honor them. • Juicy, savor them. • Kind, delight in them. • Loyal, mirror them. • Magical, fly with them. • Necessary, cultivate them. • Optimistic, support them. • Priceless, treasure them. • Quirky, enjoy them. • Rare, hold on to them. • Safe, trust them. • True, believe in them. Understanding, talk to them. • Vulnerable, embrace them. Warmhearted, value them. • Xtraordinary, recognize them. Young At Heart, play with them. • Zany, laugh with them.

30

© Meiji Stewart

How do you do—
would you like to be friends?

Janis Ian

Life is fortified
by many friendships.
To love, and to be loved,
is the greatest happiness
of existence.

Sydney Smith

If you're alive, you've got to flap your arms and legs,
you've got to jump around a lot, you've got to make a lot
of noise, because life is the very opposition of death.
...if you're quiet, you're not living.
You've got to be noisy, or at least your thoughts
should be noisy and colorful and lively.

Mel Brooks

If there's no dancing, count me out.

Emma Goldman

The optimist sees the doughnut;
the pessimist, the hole. *McLandburgh Wilson*

You must understand the whole of life, not just one little part of it. That is why you must read, that is why you must look at the skies, that is why you must sing and dance, and write poems, and suffer, and understand, for all that is life.

J . Krishnamurti

Life itself cannot give you joy unless you really will it. Life just gives you time and space—it's up to you to fill it. ·

Chinese proverb

There is more treasure in books than in all the pirates'
loot on Treasure Island and at the bottom of the
Spanish Main...and best of all, you can enjoy these
riches every day of your life. *Walt Disney*

Life is too important to be
taken seriously.

Oscar Wilde

I realize that a sense of
humor isn't for everyone.
It's only for people who
want to have fun, enjoy
life, and feel alive.

Anne Wilson Schaef

Happiness is measuring twice and cutting once.

Happiness is a present attitude—
not a future condition.

Hugh Prather

This is a the best day
the world has ever seen.
Tomorrow will be better.

R. A. Campbell

There is only one success—to be able to spend your life in your own way. *Christopher Morley*

Knowing what to say is not always necessary;
just the presence of a caring friend
can make a world of difference.

Sheri Curry

Everybody needs a friend.

Good friends always make us feel like winners,
even when we've just lost. *William Arthur Ward*

How old would you be
if you didn't know
how old you were?

Ruth Gordon

The clearest sign of wisdom
is continued cheerfulness.

Montaigne

You never know when it'll be a Kodak moment, so keep your camera ready.

The most important things
in life aren't things.

Keep my words positive: Words become my
behaviors. Keep my behaviors positive: Behaviors
become my habits. Keep my habits positive:
Habits become my values. Keep my values
positive: Values become my destiny. There is no
dress rehearsal: This is one day in your life.

Mahatma Gandhi

Every man has in himself a
continent of undiscovered
character. Happy is he who acts
the Columbus to his own soul.

Sir William Temple

Do not worry about what people
are thinking about you—for they
are not thinking about you. They
are wondering what you are
thinking about them.

Most people believe they see the world as it is. However, we really see the world as we are.

Sunshine is delicious, rain is refreshing, wind braces up, snow is exhilarating; there is no such thing as bad weather, only different kinds of good weather.

John Ruskin

It ain't no use putting up your umbrella 'til it rains.
Alice Caldwell Rice

Life is a great and wondrous mystery, and
the only thing we know that we have for sure
is what is right here right now. Don't miss it.

Leo F. Buscaglia

I have good news and I have bad news:
The bad news is that we have lost the key to
the door behind which the secret of life is hidden.
The good news is that it was never locked.

Swami Beyondananda

Don't refuse to go on an occasional wild goose chase;
that is what wild geese are made for. *Henry S. Haskins*

You can't do anything about the length of your life, but you can do something about its width and depth.

Evan Esar

We need to recapture the power of imagination; we shall find that life can be full of wonder, mystery, beauty, and joy.

Sir Harold Spencer Jones

The great pleasure in life is doing what people say you cannot do. *Walker Bagehot*

Love is the stuff that life is made of.

We are not held back by the love
we didn't receive in the past,
but by the love
we are not extending in the present.

Marianne Williamson

Happiness is a butterfly, which, when pursued, is always just beyond your grasp, but which, if you will sit down quietly, may alight upon you. *Nathaniel Hawthorne*

Expect the best. Convert problems into opportunities. Be dissatisfied with the status quo. Focus on where you want to go, instead of where you're coming from. Decide to be happy; knowing it's an attitude, a habit gained from daily practice, and not a result or payoff.

Dennis Waitley

The place to be happy is here. The time to be happy is now. The way to be happy is to help make others happy.

Why do some people always see beautiful skies and grass and lovely flowers and incredible human beings, while others are hard-pressed to find anything or any place that is beautiful? *Leo Buscaglia*

If you surrender completely
to the moments as they pass,
you live more richly those moments.

Anne Morrow Lindbergh

Joy is not in things;
it is in us.

Richard Wagner

There is nothing more remarkable in the life of Socrates than that he found time in his old age to learn to dance and play on instruments, and thought it time well spent. *Montaigne*

There is no pleasure in having
nothing to do; the fun is in having
lots to do and not doing it.

John W. Rapa

If you wait for the perfect moment
when all is safe and assured, it may
never arrive. Mountains will not be
climbed, races won, or lasting
happiness achieved.

Maurice Chevalier

I keep the telephone of my mind open to peace, harmony, health, love and abundance. Then whenever doubt, anxiety, or fear try to call me, they keep getting a busy signal and soon they'll forget my number.

Edith Armstrong

Do not keep the alabaster boxes of your love and tenderness sealed up until your friends are dead. Fill their lives with sweetness. Speak approving, cheering words while their ears can hear them and while their hearts can be thrilled by them.

Henry Ward Beecher

We create our own feelings by
the thoughts we choose to think.
We have the ability to make different choices
and create different experiences.

Louise Hay

This time, like all times, is a very good one,
if we but know what to do with it.

Ralph Waldo Emerson

I can't think of any sorrow in the world that a hot bath wouldn't help, just a little bit. *Susan Glaspell*

Each friend represents a world in us,
a world possible, not born, until they arrive,
and it is only by this meeting that
a new world is born.

Anais Nin

When you look for the good in others,
you discover the best in yourself.

Martin Walsh

United we stand, divided we fall.

Aesop

Suffering is not a
prerequisite for happiness.

Judy Tatelbaum

Be not afraid of life. Believe that
life is worth living, and your
belief will help create the fact.

William James

Anyone too busy to take care of his health is like a mechanic too busy to take care of his tools. *Spanish Proverb*

This is the true joy in life,
the being used for a purpose recognized
by yourself as a mighty one...

George Bernard Shaw

The U.S.Constitution doesn't
guarantee happiness, only the
pursuit of it. You have to catch up
with it yourself.

Benjamin Franklin

Happiness does not come from doing easy work but from
the afterglow of satisfaction that comes after the achievement
of a difficult task that demanded our best. *Theodore I. Rubin*

Half the world is on the wrong scent
in the pursuit of happiness..
They think it consists in
having and getting....
On the contrary,
it consists in giving,
and in serving...

Henry Drummond

There is nothing either good or bad,
but thinking makes it so.

William Shakespeare

When one door of happiness closes, another opens; but often we look so long at the closed door that we do not see the one which has been opened for us. *Helen Keller*

If I don't have friends,
then I ain't got nothin'.

Billie Holiday

To be able to find joy in another's joy,
that is the secret of happiness.

George Bernanos

Hold a true friend with both your hands.
Nigerian Proverb

Happiness Is...

Adventures, in self discovery. • Balance, somewhere between too little and too much. • a Choice, pass it on. Daring, to reach for the stars. • Enthusiasm, for living and loving life. • Forgiveness, carrying a grudge can be harmful to your health. • Gratitude, count your blessings, not your birthdays. • Health, honor your body, mind and spirit. • Inside, inquire within. • the Journey, not the destination. • Kindness, treat others as you would like to be treated. • Laughter, angels fly because they take themselves lightly. • Memories, a cornucopia of delights. • **N**ature, the food, the sunshine and the healer of the soul. • **O**ptimism, believe in possibilities. • **P**erseverance, without the rain there would be no rainbow. • **Q**uiet Time, slow down, breathe, and be mindful. • **R**elationships, be the love you seek. **S**ervice, the greatest gift is the gift of oneself. **T**olerance, live and help live. • **U**nconditional, no if's, and's or but's. • **V**alues, stand up for who you are and for what you believe. • **W**illingness, to have faith in everything that happens. • **X**pressing Yourself, speak your truth and the answers will come. • **Y**our Birthright, right here, right now. • **Z**zzzzzz's, a good night's sleep.

© Meiji Stewart

The joy that you give to others
is the joy that comes back to you.

John Greenleaf Whittier

A smile takes but a moment,
but it's effects sometimes last forever.

J. E. Smith

What sunshine is to flowers, smiles are to humanity. They are but trifles, to be sure, but scattered along life's pathway, the good they do is inconceivable. *Joseph Addison*

I never lose sight of the
fact that just being is fun.

Katharine Hepburn

Look at everything as though you
were seeing it either for the first or last time.
Then your time on earth will be filled with glory.

Betty Smith

Forget not that the earth delights to feel your bare feet
and the winds long to play with your hair. *Kahlil Gibran*

The trick is not how much pain you feel—
but how much joy you feel.
Anybody can feel pain.
Life is full of excuses to feel pain,
excuses not to live,
excuses, excuses, excuses.

Erica Jong

The good news is that the bad news
can be turned into good news when
you change your attitude.

Robert Schuller

For every minute you're angry,
you lose sixty seconds of happiness.

Let enthusiasm radiate in your voice, your actions,
your facial expressions, your personality,
the words you use, and the thoughts you think!

Ralph Waldo Emerson

Your success and happiness lie in you. External
conditions are the accidents of life. The great enduring
realities are love and service. Joy is the holy fire that
keeps our purpose warm and our intelligence aglow.
Resolve to keep happy, and your joy and you shall
form an invincible host against difficulty.

Helen Keller

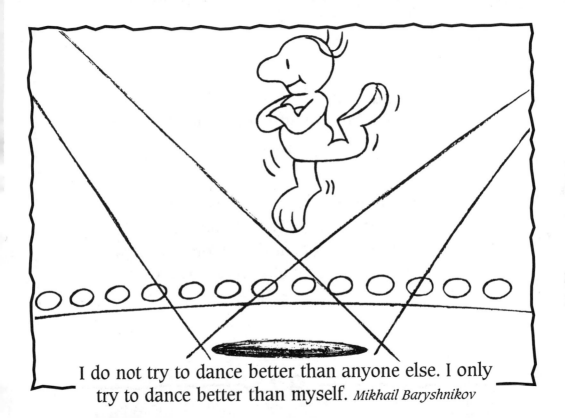

I do not try to dance better than anyone else. I only try to dance better than myself. *Mikhail Baryshnikov*

Until you make peace with who you are,
you'll never be content with what you have.

Doris Mortman

Your mind can focus on fear, worry,
problems, negativity or despair.
Or it can focus on confidence, opportunity,
solutions, optimism and success. You decide.

Don Ward

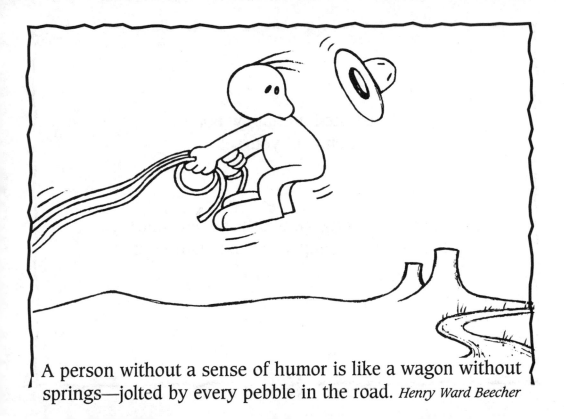

A person without a sense of humor is like a wagon without springs—jolted by every pebble in the road. *Henry Ward Beecher*

Frustrated, unhappy, bored?
Reinvent yourself.

All I can do is engage with complete sincerity.
Then, whatever happens, there is no regret.

The Dalai Lama

Happiness is an inside job.

Happiness is inward, and not outward;
and so, it does not depend on what
we have, but on what we are.

Henry Van Dyke

Learn some and think some and
draw and paint and sing and dance
and play and work every day some.

Robert Fulghum

To love what you do and feel that it matters—
how could anything be more fun?

Katharine Graham

Don't fret over what you'd do with your
time if you could live over again...
Get busy with what you have left.

You cannot prevent the birds of
sorrow from flying over your head,
but you can prevent them from
building nests in your hair.

Chinese proverb

I have always been delighted at the
prospect of a new day, a fresh try, one
more start, with perhaps a bit of magic
waiting somewhere behind the morning.

J. B. Priestley

One cannot manage too may affairs: like pumpkins in the water, one pops up while you try to hold down the other. *Chinese proverb*

Begin doing what you want to do now. We are not living in eternity. We have only this moment, sparkling like a star in our hand— and melting like a snowflake. Let us use it before it is too late.

Marie Beynon Ray

Discover day-to-day excitement.

Charles Baudelaire

Happiness... it lies in the joy of achievement, in the thrill of creative effort. *Franklin Delano Roosevelt*

If you don't like the scene you're in, if you are unhappy, if you're lonely, if you don't feel that things are happening, change your scene. Paint a new backdrop. Surround yourself with new actors. Write a new play- and if it's not a good play, get off the stage and write another one. There are millions of plays - as many as there are people.

Leo Buscaglia

You will become as small as your controlling desire; or as great as your dominant aspiration.

James Allen

Either you let your life slip away by not doing the things you want to do, or you get up and do them. *Carl Ally*

"But master," said the young student,
"In the Andes, an elderly Inca
told me that life was a sharp stone."
"That's his life," said the Himalayan sage.

Source unknown

If you do not get it from yourself,
where will you go for it?

Buddha

If you spend your whole life waiting for the storm,
you'll never enjoy the sunshine. *Morris West*

Life begets life. Energy creates
energy. It is by spending oneself
that one becomes rich.

Sarah Bernhardt

Our true age can be determined
by the ways in which we allow
ourselves to play.

Louis Walsh

Shared joy is double joy; shared sorrow is half sorrow. *Swedish Proverb*

The happiest person is the person who thinks the most interesting thoughts.

William Lyon Phelps

Slow down and enjoy life. It's not only the scenery you miss by going too fast—you also miss the sense of where you are going and why.

Eddie Cantor

Happiness comes from noticing and enjoying
the little things in life. *Barbara Ann Kipfer*

Happiness is being at peace; being with loved ones; being comfortable . . . But most of all, it's having those loved ones.

Johnny Cash

It's important to run not on the fast track, but on your track. Pretend you have only six months to live. Make three lists: the things you have to do, want to do, and neither have to do nor want to do. Then, for the rest of your life, forget everything in the third category.

Robert S. Eliot and Dennis L. Breo

To forgive is the highest, most beautiful
form of love. In return, you will receive
untold peace and happiness.

Robert Muller

Remember, happiness doesn't depend upon who you
are or what you have; it depends solely upon what you
think. So start each day by thinking of all the things
you have to be thankful for. Your future will depend
very largely on the thoughts you think today. So think
thoughts of hope and confidence and love and success.

Dale Carnegie

There's no feeling quite like the one you get when you get to the truth: You're the captain of the ship called "You." You're setting the course, the speed, and you're out there on the bridge, steering.

Carl Frederick

I like living. I have sometimes been wildly, despairingly, acutely miserable, racked with sorrow, but through it all I still know quite certainly that just to be alive is a grand thing.

Agatha Christie

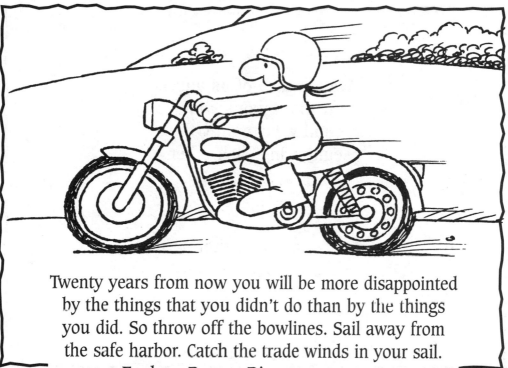

Twenty years from now you will be more disappointed
by the things that you didn't do than by the things
you did. So throw off the bowlines. Sail away from
the safe harbor. Catch the trade winds in your sail.
Explore. Dream. Discover. *Mark Twain*

We are each of us angels
with only one wing,
and we can only fly
embracing each other.

Luciano De Crescenzo

Friendship is a sheltering tree.

Samuel Taylor Coleridge

A friend is someone who comes in when the whole world has gone out. *Emilie Barnes*

In nature there are neither rewards or punishments—there are consequences.

Robert G. Ingersoll

You will never be sorry: for thinking before acting, for hearing before judging, for forgiving you enemies, for being candid and frank, for helping a fallen brother, for being honest in business, for thinking before speaking, for being loyal to your church, for standing by your principles, for stopping your ears to gossip, for bridling a slanderous tongue, for harboring only pure thoughts, for sympathizing with the afflicted, for being courteous and kind to all.

If you obey all the rules, you miss all the fun.
Katherine Hepburn

Life is what I make it,
always has been, always will be.

Grandma Moses

There are those of us who are always about to live.
We are waiting until things change, until there is
more time, until we are less tired, until we get a
promotion, until we settle down-until, until, until.
It always seems as if there is some major event
that must occur in our lives before we begin living.

George Sheehan

You never grow old until you've lost all your marvels.

Merry Browne

There is only one way to happiness and that is to cease worrying about things which are beyond the power of our will.

Epictetus

The way to happiness—keep your heart free from hate, your mind from worry, live simply, expect little, give much.

Carol Borges

To carry care to bed is to sleep with a pack on your back.
Thomas C. Haliburton

Places and circumstances never guarantee happiness. You must decide within yourself whether you want to be happy.

Robert J. Hastings

Happiness lies in the absorption in some vocation which satisfies the soul.

Sir William Osler

A musician must make music, an artist must paint, a poet must write, if he is ultimately to be at peace with himself. What a man can be, he must be. *Albert Maslow*

If you want others to be happy, practice compassion.
If you want to be happy, practice compassion.

The Dalai Lama

Thankfulness sets in motion a chain reaction that transforms people all around us, including ourselves. For no one ever misunderstands the melody of a grateful heart. Its message is universal, its lyrics transcend all earthly barriers; its music touches the heavens.

Fred Bauer

Now and then it's good to
pause in our pursuit of
happiness and just be happy.

It is better to love too many
than one too few.

John Harington

Don't evaluate your life in terms of achievements....
Instead, wake up and appreciate everything you
encounter along your path. Enjoy the flowers that are
there for your pleasure. Tune in to the sunrise, the
little children, the laughter, the rain, and the birds.
Drink it all in . . . there is no way to happiness;
happiness is the way.

Dr. Wayne W. Dyer

Recall it as often as you wish,
a happy memory never wears out.

Libbie Fudim

Stop and let the world go on
without you once in a while.

All the world is searching for joy and happiness, but these cannot be purchased for any price in any marketplace, because they are virtues that come from within, and like rare jewels must be polished, for they shine brightest in the light of faith, and in the services of brotherly love.

Lucille R. Taylor

What we call the secret of happiness is no more a secret than our willingness to choose life.

Leo F. Buscaglia

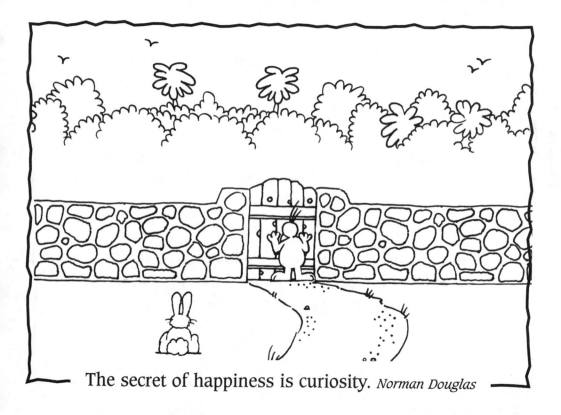

The secret of happiness is curiosity. *Norman Douglas*

I've learned, the hard way, that some poems don't rhyme, and some stories don't have a clear beginning, middle, and end. Life is about not knowing, having to change, taking the moment and making the best of it, without knowing what's going to happen next. Delicious ambiguity.

Gilda Radner

All you need in the world is love and laughter. That's all anybody needs. To have love in one hand and laughter in the other.

August Wilson

Life is as uncertain as a grapefruit's squirt.

The smile on your face is
the light in the window
that tells people that
you are at home.

I never expected to have, in my sixties,
the happiness that passed me by
in my twenties.

C.S. Lewis

It's never too late to have a happy childhood.

My friends are an oasis to me,
encouraging me to go on.
They are essential to my well-being.

Dee Brestin

The essentials for happiness are:
something to do, someone to love,
and something to hope for.

Lewis L. Dunnington

The thing that counts the most in the pursuit of happiness is choosing the right traveling companion.

If you wait until you can afford to enjoy life,
you might miss out on all the fun.

Dorothy Salone

It is only possible to live happily ever after
on a day to day basis.

Margaret Bonnano

My advice to you is not to inquire why or whither, but just enjoy your ice cream while it's on your plate—that's my philosophy. *Thornton Wilder*

I have a simple philosophy.
Fill what's empty.
Empty what's full.
And scratch where it itches.

Alice Roosevelt Longworth

Life is the greatest bargain;
we get it for nothing.

Yiddish Proverb

Make voyages.
Attempt them.
There's nothing else.

Tennessee Williams

Caring about others,
running the risk of feeling,
and leaving an impact on people
bring happiness.

Rabbi Harold Kushner

To be happy, drop the words "if only"
and substitute instead the words
"next time."

Smily Blanton, M.D.

It is not how much we have,
but how much we enjoy,
that makes happiness.

Charles Haddon Spurgeon

It is possible to own too much. A man with one watch knows what time it is; a man with two watches is never quite sure. *Lee Segall*

I found such pleasure in simple,
everyday things: a walk around the
block, just getting outside each day,
collecting leaves or seashells or pebbles,
or picking flowers in the garden.

Give yourself permission to be late sometimes.
Life is for living, not scheduling.

Linus Mundy

Happiness is having a scratch for every itch.
Ogden Nash

The motto should not be,
"Forgive one another."
Rather, "Understand one another."

Emma Goldman

Weigh the true advantages
of forgiveness and resentment
to the heart. Then choose.

Jack Kornfield

He who cannot forgive others destroys the bridge over which he himself must pass. *George Herbert*

The foolish man seeks
happiness in the distance;
the wise grows it under his feet.

James Openheim

Happiness always looks small
while you hold it in your hands,
but let it go, and you learn at
once how big and precious it is.

Maxim Gorky

Happiness is like a cat. If you try to coax it or call it, it will avoid you. It will never come. But if you pay no attention to it and go about your business, you'll find it rubbing against your legs and jumping into your lap. *William Bennett*

Life is short; live it up.

Nikita S. Khrushchev

You can't leave footprints in the
sands of time if you're sitting on your butt.
And who wants to leave buttprints
in the sands of time?

Bob Moawad

No, you never get any fun out of things you haven't done.
Ogden Nash

Above all, challenge yourself.
You may well surprise yourself
at what strengths you have,
what you can accomplish.

Cecile M. Springer

My favorite thing is to go
where I've never been.

Diane Arbus

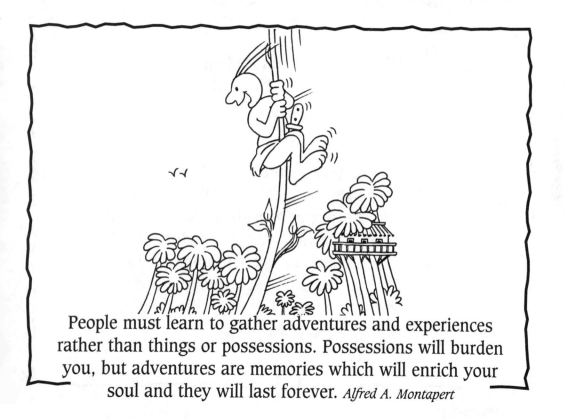

People must learn to gather adventures and experiences rather than things or possessions. Possessions will burden you, but adventures are memories which will enrich your soul and they will last forever. *Alfred A. Montapert*

The rainbow is more beautiful
than the pot at the end of it.

Hugh Prather

Live each day as you would climb a mountain. An
occasional glance toward the summit keeps the
goal in mind, but many beautiful scenes are to be
observed from each new vantage point. So climb
slowly, enjoying each passing moment; and then
the view from the summit will serve a more
rewarding climax for your journey.

Bishop Fulton J. Sheen

Yes, there is a nirvana;
it is in leading your sheep to a green pasture,
and in putting your child to sleep,
and in writing the last line of your poem.

Kahlil Gibran

Memories, important
yesterdays, were once todays.
Treasure and notice today.

Gloria Gaither

Happiness is a sunbeam . . .
When it strikes a kindred heart,
like the converged lights upon a
mirror, it reflects itself with
redoubled brightness. It is not
perfected until it is shared.

Let us go singing as far as we go:
the road will be less tedious.

Virgil

No one can whistle a symphony. It takes an orchestra to play it. *Halford E. Luccock*

We are healed from suffering
only by experiencing it to the full.

Marcel Proust

To overcome difficulties is to
experience the full delight of existence.

Arthur Schopenhauer

My barn having burned to the ground,
I can now see the moon. *Japanese Haiku*

You are never fully dressed
until you wear a smile.

Charley Willey

What really matters is
what happens in us,
not to us.

James W. Kennedy

Happiness is a habit—cultivate it.
Elbert Hubbard

If we all did the things
we are capable of doing,
we would literally astound ourselves.

Thomas A. Edison

Take risks.
You can't fall out of bed
if you sleep on the floor.

If a man does not keep pace with his companions, perhaps it is because he hears a different drummer. Let him step to the music which he hears, however measured or far away. *Henry David Thoreau*

The secret to enjoying life is to be
thankful for what each day brings.

Very little is needed to make a happy life.
It is all within yourself,
in your way of thinking.

Marcus Aurelius

If I had my life to live over, I would start barefoot earlier in the spring and stay that way later in the fall. I would go to more dances. I would ride more merry-go-rounds. I would pick more daisies. *Nadine Stair*

When Life Gives you Lemons...

and other recipes for living & loving life

Thought-provoking, attitude-changing wonderful recipes on how to make the best from the "wurst" of any situation. Accepting challenges and overcoming adversity can lead to greater self-esteem, self-acceptance and self-discovery.

A uniquely illustrated "you can if you think you can" book to empower anybody – student, co-worker, relative, friend, partner, child – to aspire to, believe in, and pursue their dreams. Go for it! Life is not a dress rehearsal.

Shoot For The Moon

Even if you miss you'll land among the stars.

It's a Jungle Out There!

The best survival kit for living and loving in the jungle of every day life. Great line drawings and timeless truths to offer hope and encouragement for anyone facing the daily challenges of our fast-paced stress-filled society.

Dare to follow your heart's desire... Dare to harvest your dreams... Dare to speak your truth... Dare to nurture your spirit... An ideal gift book to encourage anybody to aspire to, believe in and pursue dreams.

Anything is Possible

Humor & wisdom for success and prosperity

A wondrous gift for anybody interested in the well-being of children. This delightfully illustrated book uses wisdom from the ages and poignant humor to encourage everyone, especially parents and teachers, to love, cherish, and honor children.

Parenting, the ultimate adventure. Raising a child can be life's most demanding and extraordinary challenge and also its greatest happiness. A perfect gift for parents, grandparents, teachers and child care providers

Let go and let God.
Please do not feel personally,
totally, irrevocably responsible
for everything. That's my job.
Love, God.
Help someone receive
understanding, insight and
support to face life's challenges.

God has a purpose and a plan
for you that no one else can
fulfill. You are a miracle, unique
and unrepeatable. Help someone
celebrate their spiritual nature
with this collection of
empowering and loving wisdom.

"Friends Are..." on page 30 and "Happiness Is..." on page 72–73
are part of our A-Z series of gift products.
Other A-Z titles include:

- Children Are
- Children Need
- Dare To
- Fathers Are
- I Am/You Are
- Mothers Are
- Recovery Is

These unique sayings and many other empowering designs are
available on a variety of items, including bookmarks, wallet cards
and greeting cards.Please call for a complimentary catalog.

PuddleDancer PRESS™

P.O. Box 1204, Del Mar, California 92014
1-800-522-3383

Qty.	Title	Item #	Unit Cost	Total
	Relax, God is in Charge	BK01	6.95	
	Keep Coming Back	BK02	6.95	
	Children are Meant to be Seen & Heard	BK03	6.95	
	Shoot for the Moon	BK04	6.95	
	When Life Gives You Lemons...	BK05	6.95	
	It's a Jungle Out There	BK06	6.95	
	Parenting... Part Joy... Part Guerrilla Warfare	BK07	6.95	
	God Danced the Day You WereBorn	BK08	6.95	
	Happiness is an Inside Job	BK09	6.95	
	Anything is Possible	BK10	6.95	

Tax Help:
Tax on a 6.95 book is 0.54

Subtotal
Shipping & Handling (info below)
CA residents (only) add 7.75% tax
Total

PuddleDancer
PRESS

Send books to:

Name _____

Address _____

City_____ State____ Zip _____

Phone (_____)_____

Payment via:

☐ Check/money order

☐ VISA   ☐ Mastercard   ☐ AMEX

Acct#_____Exp. Date _____

Signature_____

Yes! Please send me the books indicated above. Add $2.00 shipping and handling for the first book and 50¢ for each additional book. Add $2.50 extra to the total for books shipped to Canada. Overseas orders to be paid by credit card. Allow up to four weeks for delivery. Send check or money order payable to **Keep Coming Back**. No cash or C.O.D.'s, please. Prices subject to change without notice. Quantity discount available upon request.

Mail to: Keep Coming Back, P.O. Box 1204, Del Mar, California 92014
Call: Local: 619.452.1386   Fax: 619.452.2797   Toll-free **800.522.3383**

PuddleDancer Press™

Complimentary Catalog Available
P.O. Box 1204, Del Mar, California 92014   1-800-522-3383

PuddleDancer titles available from your favorite bookstore:

Relax, God is in Charge	ISBN 0-9647349-0-7
Keep Coming Back	ISBN 0-9647349-1-5
Children are Meant to be Seen and Heard	ISBN 0-9647349-2-3
Shoot for the Moon	ISBN 0-9647349-3-1
When Life Gives You Lemons...	ISBN 0-9647349-4-X
It's a Jungle Out There!	ISBN 0-9647349-5-8
Parenting... Part Joy... Part Guerrilla Warfare	ISBN 0-9647349-6-6
God Danced the Day You Were Born	ISBN 0-9647349-7-4
Happiness is an Inside Job	ISBN 0-9647349-8-2
Anything is Possible	ISBN 0-9647349-9-0

Acknowledgements

Every effort has been made to find the copyright owner of the material used. However, there are a few quotations that have been impossible to trace, and we would be glad to hear from the copyright owners of these quotations, so that acknowledgement can be recognized in any future edition.